LATINO LIFE

SPORTS

LATINO LIFE

SPORTS

by Jeffry Jensen

Rourke Publications, Inc.

The following sources are acknowledged and thanked for the use of their photographs in this work: AP/Wide World pp. 2, 11, 13, 18, 23, 25, 27, 31, 33, 35, 36, 39, 41, 42; Ruben G. Mendoza p. 7; Elaine Querry p. 8; Robert Fried p. 14; Mark Nohl/New Mexico Economic & Tourism Department p. 16; Bob Daemmrich p. 20; Lester Sloan p. 28.

Produced by Salem Press, Inc.

∞ The paper used in these volumes conforms to the American National Standard for Permanence of Paper for Printed Library Materials, Z39.48-1984.

Library of Congress Cataloging-in-Publication Data
Jensen, Jeffry, 1950-
    Sports / by Jeffry Jensen.
        p.   cm. — (Latino life)
    ISBN 0-86625-544-3
    1. Hispanic American athletes—Biography—Juvenile literature. 2. Hispanic American athletes—History—Juvenile literature. I. Title. II. Series.
GV697.A1J47 1995   95-2029
796′.089′68073—dc20   CIP
                                                            AC

First Printing

PRINTED IN THE UNITED STATES OF AMERICA

CONTENTS

Chapter 1	The Latino Sports Tradition	6
Chapter 2	Latinos in Baseball	10
Chapter 3	Latinos in Boxing	15
Chapter 4	Latinos in Horse Racing	19
Chapter 5	Latinos in Tennis	24
Chapter 6	Latinos in Other Sports	28
Chapter 7	Prominent Latino Athletes	34
	Selected Latino Sports Figures	43
	Time Line	44
	Glossary	46
	More About Latinos and Sports	47
	Index	48

Chapter 1

THE LATINO SPORTS TRADITION

Latinos have a long and proud sports tradition. Their ancestors competed in sports activities more than two thousand years ago. The ancient people who lived in Latin America left behind buildings, statues, pottery, drawings, and other valuable artifacts. Historians and archaeologists have studied these items to learn how these people lived. These items have shown that Indian peoples played many sports long before Christopher Columbus sailed to their lands. They ran foot races, wrestled, and played a form of field hockey. They also played different types of ball games.

Scholars have divided these ball games into five main types. These types include handball, stickball, hipball, kickball, and a game called "trick" ball. People probably played these ball games in open courts or walled plazas. Juggling and gymnastics were part of the game of "trick" ball. The ball games were very popular with the Indians. They enjoyed watching the players put on an exciting show. The games often were connected to how the Indians worshiped their gods. Some of the players earned their living by participating in the games.

The ancient Maya invented the most famous Indian ball

game. Sometime around A.D. 700, the Maya began playing the rubber ball game known as *pok-ta-pok*. This game later was known as *tlachtli* to the Aztecs. *Pok-ta-pok* was usually played on a court shaped like the letter I. The court was about twenty to thirty feet wide. It could be up to 150 feet long. In the center of each side wall, a stone ring stuck out from the wall. Players competed to throw the ball through these two rings.

This game was only one of the popular hipball games in the region. Scholars know only some of the rules for playing these ancient games. People called the game "hipball" because only the players' hips and buttocks could touch the ball. The solid rubber ball had to stay in play. The defending team could earn a point even when they did not control the ball. They earned the point if the other team could not keep the ball in play. The ball was very hard and could hurt a player if he was not careful. The game ended when a player directed the ball through one of the stone

Large stone rings served as goal posts on Mayan ball courts.

rings. People in the audience gave up money and valuable objects to guess the winner of the game. The winning team would win all these items. Each team probably had two or three players.

SPANISH INFLUENCE IN THE AMERICAS

The world of the native Indians changed when Europeans started colonies in Latin America. Christopher Columbus landed in Cuba and on the island of Hispaniola in 1492. (Haiti and the Dominican Republic now share this island.) He landed on the island of Puerto Rico in 1493. Hernán Cortés and his soldiers landed in Mexico and fought the Aztec people who lived there. Cortés won battles against the Aztecs and claimed Mexico for Spain in 1521. Another Spanish soldier led his army into Peru. His name was Francisco Pizarro. Pizarro and his troops destroyed the native Inca civilization of Peru during the 1500's. The Spanish soldiers brought new games in the areas they conquered. They would not allow the native Indians to play their original ball games.

The Spanish eventually brought bullfighting to Latin America. People in Spain had fought against bulls since ancient times. The word for bullfight in the Spanish language is *corrida*. The person who fights and kills the bull is a *matador*. Matadors are considered heroes in the countries that allow bullfights. The first bullfights were held in the New World during the mid-1500's. Mexico City is known as the site of the world's largest bullring in the 1990's. The city has a stadium that seats more than 50,000 people.

Spanish settlers brought the sport of *jai alai* to Mexico and other Spanish colonies. This ball game began in the Basque region of Spain. This region is near Spain's border with France. Playing jai alai is like playing handball. There is one important difference. Jai alai players use a large scooped-out paddle instead of using their bare hands. They use this paddle to catch or fling the ball against a walled court.

Two other important sports came to Latin America during the 1860's. British sailors introduced the game of *soccer* in South America. Soccer is known in Spanish as *fútbol*. Soccer soon became very popular throughout the region. Merchant marines from the United States introduced the game of baseball in Cuba. Baseball soon spread to the rest of the Caribbean and to Central America. Other sports eventually became popular. These sports include cycling, horse racing, boxing, automobile racing, basketball, and tennis.

Chapter 2

LATINOS IN BASEBALL

Cubans first learned to play baseball during the 1860's. Baseball had become a popular sport in Cuba by the late 1870's. People in the Central American country of Nicaragua had organized baseball leagues by the 1890's. The United States bought and sold many products in Latin America during this time. Americans who came to Latin America spread the game of baseball. People in Cuba, Nicaragua, the Dominican Republic, Panama, Venezuela, and Colombia began to play baseball.

A game played in Cuba in ancient times resembled the modern game of baseball. Players used a stick, a ball, and some stone bases. It is not surprising that baseball became so popular in Cuba. The professional Cuban Baseball League (Liga de Béisbol Profesional Cubana) was founded in 1878.

"Street" baseball had become popular in parts of Mexico by the 1890's. The Yucatán region built its first authentic baseball stadium in 1904. This stadium was modeled on Ebbets Field, the home of the Brooklyn Dodgers in New York. Latin Americans began to come to the United States for the chance to play professional baseball.

Players from the United States sometimes started playing in the Latin American baseball leagues. They did this to polish their skills before returning home to major league competition. Other players also traveled to Latin America. In the United States, it was hard for African Americans to get jobs playing professional baseball. Some of them chose to play on baseball teams in Latin America instead.

LATINO BALLPLAYERS IN THE UNITED STATES

One black player who came to the United States was Esteban Bellán. He was a native of Cuba whose ancestors came from Africa. In 1871, he began playing for the Troy Haymakers in New York. Bellán was the first Latino to play major league baseball in the United States. Bellán's major league career ended in 1873 while he was playing for the New York Mutuals. White baseball owners and players stopped allowing black people to play on professional teams. No other black people from Cuba were allowed to play in the major leagues until 1947.

Latinos who had light-colored skin eventually were allowed to play in the major leagues. Some American players and fans disliked these players because of their Latino heritage. Until 1911, only two Latino players besides

Juan Marichal of the San Francisco Giants is one of many Latino ballplayers who were born in the Dominican Republic.

Bellán competed in the major leagues. One of the players was Luis Castro, a native of Colombia. He played for the Philadelphia A's in 1901. Castro was the first Latino from South America to play in the major leagues. The other player was Vicente "Sandy" Nava. He played from 1882 to 1886 with teams in Baltimore, Maryland, and Providence, Rhode Island.

In 1911, two Cuban players signed to play baseball in the National League. Their names were Rafael Almeida and Armando Marsans. They both played for the Cincinnati Reds and were fine baseball players. Soon, major league teams started recruiting other Cuban players. Miguel González signed with the Boston Braves as a catcher in 1912. He went on to play in the major leagues for seventeen years. González became a coach after he stopped playing baseball. He was the first Latino to coach in the major leagues. He coached for the National League's St. Louis Cardinals for fourteen seasons.

The Boston Braves signed another player from Cuba in 1914. He was a pitcher named Adolfo Luque. Luque learned how to handle the insults he received from white players and fans. Luque pitched for twenty seasons with several teams. He had a record of 193 wins and 179 losses and a lifetime *earned run average* (ERA) of 3.24. There were some major league teams that gave Latin American ballplayers more chances to play. The Washington Senators had nineteen players from Latin American countries on its team between 1939 and 1947.

One famous Latino played for the New York Yankees during the early decades of the twentieth century. His name was Vernon "Lefty" Gomez. He was born in California and learned to pitch left-handed. Gomez began playing for the Yankees in 1930. He won 189 games during his brilliant career.

During the 1940's, a new baseball league was formed in Mexico. It was called the Mexican League. Owners of professional baseball clubs in the United States did not like

In 1937, Vernon "Lefty" Gomez led the American League in wins, strikeouts, and earned run average (ERA).

this new league. They tried to keep all major league players from competing in the Mexican League.

BLACK LATINO BALLPLAYERS

Latino ballplayers of African descent could not play in the major leagues. Many of them played in the segregated Negro Leagues. Some Negro League athletes played baseball in the Latin American leagues during the winter. After 1947, major league baseball teams began signing black players to play for them. In 1949, a Cuban-born black player signed a contract to play in the major leagues. Saturnino Orestes Armas Miñoso was born in Havana, Cuba. He earned the nickname "Minnie." Miñoso had first played in the United States with the Negro Leagues for several years. He started with the Cleveland Indians in 1949 and played in the major leagues for fifteen years.

A young Puerto Rican named Roberto Clemente began his major league career in 1955. He signed a contract to play with the Pittsburgh Pirates. Clemente was a talented

Latino last names are a common sight on the backs of uniforms worn by many of today's professional baseball players.

player who could field and hit very well. Some players and fans disliked Clemente because he was a Latino of African descent. He tried to ignore the mean comments these people made. Clemente became known for always helping others in need. He died in a plane crash while trying to bring supplies to earthquake victims in Nicaragua in 1972.

Many Latinos have looked to baseball as a way to success. Many of them grew up in poor families. Professional baseball offered salaries that allowed Latino players to help their families and friends. Several Latin American countries have produced talented baseball players. These countries include Cuba, the Dominican Republic, Puerto Rico, Mexico, and Venezuela. People in these countries did not have to buy fancy equipment to enjoy playing baseball. That is also why baseball became popular with many Latinos born in the United States.

Eventually, major league teams began hiring Latino ballplayers to work as team managers. There were three Latino managers of major league teams during the 1993 baseball season. They included Cito Gaston of the Toronto Blue Jays, Felipe Alou of the Montreal Expos, and Tony Perez of the Cincinnati Reds.

Chapter 3

LATINOS IN BOXING

Boxing has existed since ancient times. The Greeks and Romans used boxing matches to help celebrate holidays. The fights at these holiday celebrations were very popular. The fights were dangerous because no one had established rules for boxing. Fighters could lose their lives in a boxing match. That is why boxing was not allowed for hundreds of years in some countries. It became popular again in seventeenth century England. The fighters had to be fit in order to survive the boxing matches. They needed to be skilled and also had to have endurance and courage.

The English are considered the inventors of modern boxing. The Marquess of Queensberry established rules for boxing in 1867. He wanted the fights to be fair to the participants. The new rules made boxers use padded gloves and fight in a boxing ring on a canvas floor. Boxers fought during a certain number of rounds that lasted three minutes. There was a one-minute rest period between each round.

American audiences learned about boxing by watching visiting English fighters in the 1850's and 1860's. People in Latin American countries began watching boxing in the late 1800's. They learned about boxing through their contacts with the English and with Americans.

LATINOS LEARN ABOUT BOXING

Latin America countries had their own boxing matches by the early 1900's. Many Latin American countries had special clubs that focused on organized boxing. Working-class people and poor people became boxing fans around this time. They believed that professional boxing provided a way to achieve success. These fans admired the courage of professional fighters. Many boxers risked being hurt or permanently injured. They were willing to take these risks to become champions in their chosen sport. Some boxers went on to become national heroes.

Boxing is very popular among Latinos in the United States. In boxing, fighters compete against other people whose weights are close to theirs. Most Latino boxers have competed in the lighter body weight classes. Latino boxers have become famous for being tough competitors. Many of them have used their speed to increase their chances of winning bouts. Many Latino fighters were too poor to pay

Two young Latino boxers compete in a match at the Whole Enchilada Fiesta in Las Cruces, New Mexico.

for private boxing lessons. They took advantage of the free boxing lessons offered by boys' clubs and police athletic leagues. Other young Latinos became interested in boxing while serving in the military. Boxing offered a way for these Latinos to achieve fame and financial success.

PROFESSIONAL BOXING

By the 1900's, the center of professional boxing had shifted to the United States. One of the first Latin American fighters to become famous was born in Argentina. His name was Luis Angel Firpo. Firpo became famous in the United States when he fought Jack Dempsey in 1923. Firpo lost the heavyweight championship. Even so, he became a hero to people in Argentina. People around the world realized that Argentina could produce a great athlete.

Other Latin American fighters decided to move to the United States to pursue boxing careers. One of the first boxers to do this was Eligio Sardiñas. He was born in Havana, Cuba, in 1910. He became a boxer and was known by the nickname "Kid Chocolate." He started boxing in Cuba before moving to New York in 1928. Kid Chocolate fought more than one hundred fights during his career in the United States. He was elected to the Boxing Hall of Fame in 1959.

LATINO BOXING CHAMPIONS

Sixto Escobar was the first Puerto Rican boxer to win a world championship. He competed in the *bantamweight* division. The word "bantam" is another name for a small rooster or fighting cock. That is how Escobar earned the nickname "the Barceloneta Fighting Cock." In 1934, he defeated Baby Casanova to win the National Boxing Association (NBA) bantamweight title. Escobar defeated Tony Marino in 1936 to win the world bantamweight title. Escobar became a national hero in Puerto Rico. A stadium in the Puerto Rican capital of San Juan was named in Escobar's honor. Puerto Rico has produced other

world-class boxers. These fighters include Carlos Ortiz and José Luis Torres. They were the second and third Puerto Rican fighters to win world championship titles.

There have been more than 150 world champion fighters from Latin American countries. Some of these famous boxers include Roberto Durán from Panama, Alexis Arguello from Nicaragua, and Vicente Saldívar and Julio César Chávez from Mexico.

Many Latino boxing champions have grown up in the United States. Manuel Ortiz was the best amateur *flyweight* fighter in Southern California by 1937. He grew up in Corona, California, and won Golden Gloves and national titles. Ortiz won the bantamweight title during his professional boxing career. Other Latinos who captured world boxing titles include *welterweight* Carlos Palomino, *featherweight* and junior-lightweight Bobby Chacón, lightweight Armando Ramos, flyweight Michael Carbajal, and junior-lightweight and lightweight Oscar de la Hoya.

Boxer Roberto Durán raises his glove to celebrate his victory over Sugar Ray Leonard on June 20, 1980.

Chapter 4

Latinos in Horse Racing

Spanish conquistadors brought horses with them to the Americas in the sixteenth century. The sight of these Spanish soldiers riding on horseback stunned the Aztecs of Mexico. The horses and riders looked like one creature to the Aztecs. The Aztecs thought the riders were gods. Aztecs also worshiped the horse.

Spanish settlers brought more horses to North and South America. The settlers established large ranches, known as *haciendas* or *ranchos*. They raised cattle for meat on their ranches. People worked and played sports on horseback on the ranches. The mixing of Spanish and Indian customs led to the idea of using the horse in sporting competitions. The events in these competitions became part of the modern rodeo.

The Cowboy Heritage of the Vaqueros

In seventeenth century Mexico, people who could handle horses skillfully became known as *vaqueros*. "Vaquero" is a Spanish word meaning cowboy. Most of the vaqueros were of mixed Spanish and Indian heritage and were known as *mestizos* (a Spanish word for mixed blood or parentage). Other cowboys were known as *charros* on the large Spanish ranches. They took pride in their ability to do exciting tricks while riding their horses.

The charros became the models for the North American

cowboy. They wore special outfits when they rode their horses. These outfits included colorful neck scarves known as *bandanas* and special leg coverings that became known as *chaps*. Their Spanish term for their braided rope—*la reata*—became the basis for the English word "lariat."

The charros invented games and contests where they showed their knowledge and skill at handling horses. Events held at a *charrería* (a Spanish word meaning contest in Mexico) included the *correr el gallo* (running the rooster), horse racing, wild horse and bull riding, steer and horse roping, and bulldogging (wrestling a steer to the ground and tying its hooves together). In the *correr el gallo*, the charros picked up a small object from the ground while riding their horses at full speed. The *charrería* is still a popular sport in Mexico. By the early 1920's, the American form of the *charrería*—the rodeo—had become a sport. It is also

Three young women ride sidesaddle as they compete in a **charreada,** *or rodeo, held in San Antonio, Texas.*

popular among people of Mexican heritage living in the American Southwest.

One of the most famous charros was Vicente Oropeza. He was born in Mexico and first competed in the United States in San Antonio, Texas, in July of 1891. Oropeza toured throughout the United States for more than ten years with "Buffalo" Bill Cody's Wild West Show. Oropeza became the first cowboy to win the World Championship of Trick and Fancy Roping in 1900.

THE ROOTS OF HORSE RACING

Horse racing is one of the oldest organized sports in North America. The English first introduced horse racing to the American colonies. The first British governor of New York was Colonel Richard Nicolls. He wanted to have horse racing in the colony. A race course was built near Hempstead, New York, in 1665. It was called "Newmarket Course."

English settlers brought over thoroughbreds or horses specially bred for racing. The first of these horses came to the colony of Virginia sometime around 1730. Horse owners began using professional jockeys to race their horses during the eighteenth century. The owners realized that their horses could run faster if the jockeys were small and weighed less than 120 pounds. Horse racing had become a popular sport in the United States by the 1800's. A crowd of 60,000 people watched a race in 1823 held at the Union Race Course on Long Island, New York. This was the first large crowd to view an American sporting event. In 1875, the first Kentucky Derby was held at Churchill Downs racetrack in Louisville, Kentucky.

Horse racing was introduced in South America during the late 1800's. The first organized English-style horse race was run in Chile on September 20, 1867. An English-style race had already been held in Argentina in 1826. People in Argentina founded a Jockey Club in 1882. There were several horse racing organizations in Chile by the 1920's.

These organizations included the Club Hípico, the Hipódromo Chile, and the Valparaíso Sporting Club. Horse racing became even more popular in South America during the early decades of the twentieth century.

During the 1940's, horse owners in the United States began hiring jockeys who had grown up in Latin America. Some of the first Latin American jockeys who came to the United States were Mike Villena from Chile, Mannie Ycaza and Braulio Baeza from Panama, and Avelino Gómez from Cuba. There were approximately three thousand jockeys racing in the United States by the early 1990's. It was estimated that more than twenty-five percent of the jockeys riding in U.S. races were Latinos.

LIFE AS A PROFESSIONAL JOCKEY

Life is very hard for a professional jockey. Only some one hundred jockeys make more than $15,000 per year. A person must have talent and work hard to be a successful professional jockey. The best jockeys also have good agents who find owners who will hire the jockeys to ride. Jockeys are paid to win races. A jockey is paid a minimum fee for simply riding. Sometimes a jockey will earn extra money by exercising the horses. Jockeys finish in first place usually earn ten percent of the owner's winnings as a bonus. Jockeys who finish in second or third place are awarded five percent of the owner's winnings.

Even if they win very few races, jockeys must spend their own money to compete. They are responsible for buying their own personal riding equipment, paying their agents, and contributing money to the Jockey's Guild for life insurance and the guild's injury fund. This insurance is important because horse racing is a very dangerous sport. Jockeys have been killed during horse races. Others have been seriously injured or paralyzed when they were thrown from their horses during a race.

Two of the most successful Latino jockeys in the history of horse racing are Ángel Cordero, Jr., from Puerto Rico and Laffit Pincay, Jr., from Panama. Pincay had won more than 7,800 races in his career by 1994. He was ranked second on the all-time victory list behind Willie Shoemaker. Cordero retired from horse racing in 1992 with more than 7,000 wins and was ranked third on the all-time victory list.

Jockey Ángel Cordero, Jr., rode Spend a Buck to victory in the 1985 Kentucky Derby.

Chapter 5

LATINOS IN TENNIS

Tennis is a popular game all over the world. It can be played by people of all ages. Millions of people play tennis to relax, but there are only a few hundred players who make a living in professional tennis. Historians believe that the French probably invented the game of tennis during the twelfth or thirteenth century. An English colonel is credited by historians for inventing the modern game of tennis in 1873. His name was Walter C. Wingfield. Before long, tennis became England's most popular outdoor sport.

Mary Ewing Outerbridge introduced tennis to the United States in 1874. The United States National Lawn Tennis Association (which has been changed to the United States Tennis Association) was started in 1881. The association sponsored its first men's tournament in the same year. The tournament was played in Newport, Rhode Island. The United States, Great Britain, and France produced the majority of the best tennis players during the early decades of the 1900's.

Tennis first began as a game played by the well-to-do. Talented players had access to tennis lessons. They usually were members of private clubs. Club members could practice and play against other talented players. People who could not afford private club fees started playing tennis when public tennis courts were built. In the 1930's, players could go to local public parks and find tennis courts.

A TRADITION OF EXCELLENCE

One of the best tennis players of all time was born in Los Angeles, California. His name was Pancho Gonzales. He played tennis on public courts because his Mexican American family could not afford to pay for private tennis lessons. In 1948 and 1949, he won the United States National Championship. Gonzales traveled around the world during the 1950's and into the 1960's, playing on the professional tennis tour. He was one of the pioneers of professional tennis. Gonzales was a tough competitor who was exciting to watch. He proved that a world-class player did not have to grow up perfecting his skills in private clubs.

A Latin American tennis player moved to the United States to attend the University of Miami in the 1940's. He was Pancho Segura of Ecuador. Segura was the Intercollegiate tennis champion for three years (1943-1945). Segura became known as "Little Pancho" to distinguish him from the tall Pancho Gonzales. Segura was a very unusual tennis player since he stroked the ball with a two-handed *backhand* and *forehand* grip. In addition to being a great tennis player, he became a successful coach.

After turning professional in 1946, Pancho Segura won three consecutive singles titles in 1950, 1951, and 1952.

During the 1950's and 1960's, Latin America produced more tennis champions. Alex Olmedo from Peru was a leading tennis player. Olmedo attended college in the United States at the University of Southern California (USC). He was chosen as a member of the United States Davis Cup team. He helped the team win the Davis Cup competition in 1958. Some people did not think he should be on the team, since he was not an American citizen. Olmedo went on to win the world's most respected championship in 1959. This championship is known as Wimbledon, in honor of the town in England where it is played. In 1963, another Latin American player won the United States National Championship. He was Rafael Osuna from Mexico. Manuel Santana became the first tennis player from Spain to win the United States National Championship in 1965. He went on to win the Wimbledon title in 1966.

OUTSTANDING LATINAS IN TENNIS

A tennis player from Brazil won both the Wimbledon title and the United States National Championship in 1959. Her name was Maria Bueno. Bueno won Wimbledon again in 1960 and 1964. She was the top-ranked woman tennis player in the world between 1959 and 1960. Bueno also won the United States Championship in 1963, 1964, and 1966.

One of the most successful Latino women ever to compete on the tennis courts was Rosemary Casals. She was born in San Francisco, California, in 1948. Casals was an excellent singles player, but she made her reputation playing doubles with the legendary Billie Jean King. The team of Casals and King won fifty-six professional tennis titles, including seven Wimbledon titles in women's doubles.

THE TRADITION CONTINUES

Latino tennis players from various countries have become popular to Latino audiences in the United States because tennis is such an international event. Raul Ramírez was born in Mexico, but came to the United States to attend

Dominican-born athlete Mary Joe Fernández has been playing tennis professionally since the age of fourteen.

college at USC. He and his doubles partner, Brian Gottfried, were almost unbeatable at the college level. They went on to become one of the best doubles teams in professional tennis. One of the most popular international Latino tennis players was Guillermo Vilas from Argentina. He was one of the leading professional tennis players during the 1970's. Other international Latino tennis players who have become outstanding professional competitors include Gabriela Sabatini from Argentina, Arantxa Sánchez-Vicario and Sergi Bruguera from Spain, and Andrés Gómez from Ecuador, to name only a few examples.

One of the leading American women players during the 1990's is Mary Joe Fernández. She was born in the Dominican Republic and moved with her family to the United States when she was only six months old. She and Gigi Fernández of Puerto Rico teamed up to represent the United States at the 1992 Summer Olympics in Barcelona, Spain. They won the gold medal in women's doubles competition.

Chapter 6

LATINOS IN OTHER SPORTS

In addition to the sports already covered, Latinos have made their mark in football, golf, soccer, and track and field. It was difficult for Latinos to participate in any sports other than baseball, boxing, and horse racing before the 1950's. Most Latinos are descended from Spanish and American Indian ancestors who were of average height. That may be one reason why few Latinos have excelled at basketball, where size is very important.

EDUCATION AND SPORTS

Latinos have had other problems succeeding in certain sports. In some sports, athletes need to attend college to

Extracurricular sports help encourage young Latinos to finish their education. Here, several Latino boys compete in a local high school track meet in Los Angeles.

prepare for professional competition. Unfortunately, the percentage of Latinos who do not finish high school is very large. Gradually, more Latino families have begun to find better-paying jobs. This change has encouraged Latino athletes from these families to complete high school and attend college. More Latinos have gone on to compete in professional football, basketball, and track and field.

SOCCER

Soccer is the most popular sport in the world outside of the United States. It is the national sport of many Latin American countries. Soccer's popularity in Latin American countries has made it equally popular in Latino communities in the United States. The most famous soccer player of all time is Pelé from Brazil. He helped his country win soccer's international championship, known as the World Cup, three times. Pelé came to the United States in 1975 to play for the New York Cosmos of the North American Soccer League (NASL). He helped make soccer popular in the United States.

LATINOS IN PROFESSIONAL FOOTBALL

Some Latinos who had developed excellent kicking skills in soccer began competing in football as *placekickers*. Many members of the Zendejas family have become field goal kickers in the National Football League (NFL). Tony Zendejas is probably the best-known kicker. His brother Marty and his cousins Luis, Max, and Joaquín have also played for NFL teams. The most famous Latino *quarterback* is Jim Plunkett. His mother was of Mexican heritage. Jim Plunkett was a star quarterback at Stanford University during the 1960's and won the Heisman Trophy. He played football with the Oakland Raiders. He led the Raiders to two Super Bowl victories during his career.

Another Latino player, Tom Flores, played for the Kansas City Chiefs. He played for the Chiefs when they won the Super Bowl on January 11, 1970. Flores became a professional football coach after he retired from playing. He coached the Raiders to victories in the Super Bowl games held in 1981 and 1984. Flores went on to become coach and then president of the Seattle Seahawks.

Other Latinos who have excelled in professional football include Manny Fernández and Anthony Muñoz. Fernández played for the Miami Dolphins from 1968 to 1977. He was an outstanding defensive tackle and helped the Dolphins to win Super Bowl championships in 1973 and 1974. Fernández was named to the All-Time Greatest Super Bowl All-Star Team. Muñoz played professional football for the Cincinnati Bengals from 1980 to 1992. Muñoz was selected to the Pro Bowl several times during his career.

THE LATINO TRADITION IN GOLF

In general, the sport of golf has seen few Latinos rise to the top. For many years, only members of private country clubs could play on golf courses. These private clubs were expensive to join. The clubs did not allow African Americans or Latinos to become members. Golf itself is an expensive game. A player must purchase his or her own golf clubs, balls, and special shoes in order to compete. Eventually, many cities began to build public golf courses where anyone who could pay an entry fee could play. Latinos who could afford the equipment and the course fees could play golf on the public courses.

There have been a few Latino golfers who have become household names. Lee Trevino grew up in Dallas, Texas. He left school at a young age to work at the local country club. The country club allowed Trevino to play golf at night as a reward for his hard work. He joined the Professional Golfers Association (PGA) in 1966. Trevino won most of the major golf tournaments while he played as a professional.

There was another Latino golfer who was playing at about the same time as Trevino. His name was Juan Rodríguez, and he went by the nickname "Chi Chi." He was born on October 23, 1935, in Río Piedras, Puerto Rico.

He earned money as a boy by working on golf courses as a *caddy* for tourists who took vacations in Puerto Rico. Eventually, he learned to play golf well and began to compete as a professional golfer. When he turned fifty, he began competing on the Senior Tour.

Chi Chi Rodríguez earned more than three million dollars as a professional golfer by the early 1990's. He gave some of his award money to charities. He also founded the Chi Chi Rodriguez Youth Foundation, located in Clearwater, Florida. In the years since Rodríguez and Trevino have played, Latino golfers from other countries have become famous. They include Seve Ballesteros and José-María Olazabal from Spain.

Latino golfer Chi Chi Rodríguez used some of his prize money to establish a charity to help children in Florida.

Another Latino golfer who has established an impressive reputation as a professional is Nancy Lopez. She was born in Torrance, California, but grew up in New Mexico. She decided to learn golf after watching her father when he played. Later, she got a scholarship to attend college at Tulsa University in Oklahoma. She began her career as a professional golfer in 1977 and won many tournaments.

LATINO TRACK STARS

One of the outstanding Latinos to compete in track and field events has been Alberto Salazar. Salazar was born in Havana, Cuba, and came to the United States when he was young. He finished high school before attending the University of Oregon. Salazar was an excellent runner in college. After he graduated from college, he competed in the New York Marathon and won it on several occasions. Doug Padilla and Joe Falcon are other Latinos who also competed as runners for college teams.

A WORLD-CLASS SWIMMER

Pablo Morales became one of top swimmers in the world. His parents left Cuba in 1956, and moved to Chicago. Pablo was born there in 1964, and his family moved to Santa Clara, California, in 1966. Morales won the Junior National in the 100- and 200-meter butterfly in 1981. He finished high school and attended Stanford University. He won eleven National Collegiate Athletic Association (NCAA) championship events during his four years at Stanford. No other NCAA swimmer had ever won so many events.

Morales competed in the 100-meter butterfly at the 1984 Summer Olympics in Los Angeles, California. He had hoped to win the gold, but won the silver medal instead. He was disappointed four years later when he did not make it on the U.S. Olympic swimming team. Morales went on to continue his education by attending law school at Cornell University in New York. He did not give up on swimming. Morales took time off from law school to prepare for the

1992 Summer Olympics in Barcelona, Spain. He wanted to succeed to honor his mother, who had died of cancer. In Barcelona, he competed in the 100-meter butterfly and finally won the gold medal.

Chapter 7

PROMINENT LATINO ATHLETES

ROBERTO CLEMENTE (1934-1973)

Born on August 18, 1934, in Carolina, Puerto Rico, Roberto Clemente witnessed his parents' struggle to make a living. As a child, he learned how to bat by hitting tin cans with a stick. Roberto played baseball in high school and also threw the javelin on the track team. He was a fine natural athlete, but baseball was his first love.

Clemente first signed to play baseball for the Santurce Crabbers of the Puerto Rican league. The Brooklyn Dodgers were impressed with his skills. They offered Clemente ten thousand dollars as a bonus to sign a contract with them. He was later drafted by the Pittsburgh Pirates in 1955. Clemente helped the Pirates win the World Series in 1960 and in 1971. Clemente won the National League batting title four times—1961, 1964, 1965, and 1967. He was also an outstanding defensive outfielder who was awarded the Gold Glove twelve times. Clemente had a lifetime batting average of .317 and a total of 3,000 hits. He was admitted to the National Baseball Hall of Fame in 1973.

Clemente played for the Pirates until his death in 1972. He was killed when the plane he was riding in crashed into the Atlantic Ocean in December of 1972. He was the honorary

Baseball Hall of Famer Roberto Clemente learned to play baseball in his native Puerto Rico.

chair of the Nicaraguan Relief Committee and had decided to travel there himself. The plane was carrying relief supplies to help the victims of an earthquake in Managua, Nicaragua.

FERNANDO VALENZUELA (BORN 1960)

Fernando Valenzuela was born on November 1, 1960, in Etchohuaquila, Mexico. He loved baseball and had become a star pitcher in Mexico by 1978. Fernando was named Rookie of the Year in the Mexican League in 1979. He signed a contract to play for the Los Angeles Dodgers of the National League that same year. Fernando moved up from the Dodgers' minor league teams by the end of the 1980 season. He began pitching for the major league team in Los Angeles.

The next season was a dream year for Fernando Valenzuela, even though the season ended early because of a baseball strike. He led the league in strikeouts (180) and in shutouts (8). Large crowds came to the ballpark to watch

Pitcher Fernando Valenzuela was the first player to be honored as Rookie of the Year and winner of the Cy Young Award in the same year.

him pitch. Reporters called his popularity with baseball fans "Fernandomania." The Dodgers went on to win the World Series in 1981. He also became the first baseball player to win both the Cy Young and Rookie of the Year awards in the same year. In 1986, Valenzuela led the National League with twenty-one victories.

Soon, Valenzuela began having pain in his left shoulder. It was hard for him to pitch with his left arm as well as he had before. The Dodgers decided to release him from his contract after the 1990 season. He continued to struggle to regain his old form. Valenzuela signed contracts in the American League instead. He pitched briefly for the

California Angels and later for the Baltimore Orioles. He even returned to Mexico to pitch in the Mexican League. Valenzuela returned to the National League in 1994, when he got a chance to pitch for the Philadelphia Phillies.

Oscar de la Hoya (born 1973)

Oscar de la Hoya was born on February 4, 1973, in East Los Angeles, California. His father, Joel de la Hoya, worked as a shipping and receiving clerk. Oscar's grandfather had been a boxer in Mexico, and when Oscar's father was young, he had been a professional boxer. Joel de la Hoya entered Oscar in a Pee-Wee boxing tournament when Oscar was six years old. Growing up in a dangerous neighborhood, Oscar found refuge in organized boxing.

Oscar de la Hoya won the 119-pound Junior Olympic title in 1988, when he was fifteen years old. He became the 125-pound Golden Gloves champion in 1989. De la Hoya won his first gold medal at the Goodwill Games in 1990. Unfortunately, his mother Cecilia died from breast cancer in October of that year. He continued to attend school and was graduated from Garfield High School in 1991. De la Hoya competed at the 1992 Summer Olympics in Barcelona, Spain, in the 132-pound weight category. He went on to win the only gold medal in boxing received by the United States team. Oscar de la Hoya made his professional boxing debut in November of 1992. He defeated Jorge Páez in 1994 to capture the World Boxing Organization's (WBO) lightweight title.

Ángel Cordero, Jr. (born 1942)

Ángel Cordero, Jr., was born on November 8, 1942, in Santurce, Puerto Rico. He was destined for horse racing. The Cordero family was famous in Puerto Rico for their ability as jockeys. Ángel became a leading jockey in Puerto Rico before moving to the United States to compete. He began racing in the United States in 1965. Cordero was one of the leading jockeys on the circuit by 1968.

Ángel Cordero rode Cannonade to victory in the Kentucky Derby in 1974. He went on to become the leading money-winner among professional jockeys in 1976. He rode Bold Forbes to victory at the Kentucky Derby and at the Belmont Stakes during the same year. Cordero was a very aggressive rider. Owners admired his ability to guide horses to a powerful finish. Cordero retired from racing in 1992. He won more than seven thousand races during his career. This record placed him third on the all-time win list among jockeys.

RICHARD ALONZO "PANCHO" GONZALES (BORN 1928)

Pancho was born Richard Alonzo Gonzales on May 9, 1928, in Los Angeles, California. He was the son of Mexican immigrants who had come to the United States looking for a better life. His family called him Pancho. He learned to play tennis on public courts in Los Angeles. He was not able to afford tennis lessons, but he had natural talent and was eager to improve. These qualities helped him become one of the best players in the history of tennis.

Pancho Gonzales played in his first major tennis tournament when he was nineteen years old. He was six feet, three inches tall. Gonzales was also a fiery competitor who had a powerful tennis serve. He won the United States National Championship in 1948 and 1949. He decided to become a professional tennis player in 1950. Gonzales traveled around the world on the professional tennis tour during the 1950's and into the 1960's. In 1970, Gonzales became the tennis director at Caesar's Palace, a resort hotel in Las Vegas, Nevada. He was elected to the National Lawn Tennis Hall of Fame in 1968.

NANCY LOPEZ (BORN 1957)

Nancy Lopez was born on January 6, 1957, in Torrance, California. She learned how to play golf from her father when she was eight years old. Nancy began winning youth

Golfer Nancy Lopez talks to her shot during a golf tournament on the Ladies Professional Golf Association tour.

tournaments in New Mexico. After finishing high school, she attended Tulsa University, where she was named a college All-American. Lopez decided to become a professional golfer in 1977 and joined the Ladies Professional Golf Association (LPGA). She had an outstanding season and was named the Rookie of the Year. She won the LPGA Championship in 1978 and again in 1985. Lopez took time off from golf in the late 1980's to care for her young daughters. She later returned to the women's professional golf tour and won the LPGA Championship in 1989. Lopez was named to the LPGA Hall of Fame in 1987.

LEE TREVINO (BORN 1939)

Lee Trevino was born on December 1, 1939, in Dallas, Texas. He grew up in a poor Mexican American family. His family lived near the Glen Lakes Country Club. Lee began learning how to play golf when he was six years old. After dropping out of school to help support his family, he began working at the club. He helped take care of the grass on the golf course. He sometimes worked as a caddy, helping to carry the club members' golf bags. Between 1957 and 1961, Lee Trevino served in the United States Marines. He returned home after he completed his service with the Marines and found work as a golf instructor and club professional.

Trevino began playing on the Professional Golfers Association (PGA) tour in 1966. He had an outstanding year and was named Rookie of the Year in 1967. He won the prestigious U.S. Open tournament in 1968. Trevino captured the championship titles at the U.S., British, and Canadian Opens in 1971. As a result of these victories, Trevino was named PGA Player of the Year, *Sports Illustrated* Sportsman of the Year, and Associated Press Athlete of the Year. Trevino went on to win the 1972 British Open and the PGA Championship in 1974 and 1984. Lee Trevino was always a popular player. He joined the PGA Senior Tour after his fiftieth birthday in 1989. He has made money from endorsing Cadillac cars, Spalding golf products, and La Victoria Mexican food products on television. Trevino was named to the PGA/World Golf Hall of Fame in 1981.

JAMES WILLIAM "JIM" PLUNKETT, JR. (BORN 1947)

Jim Plunkett was born on December 5, 1947. He grew up in Santa Clara, California. His parents were legally blind. They had met at a special school in New Mexico before they were married. Jim was a very good football player in high school and went on to play football at Stanford University. He was named an All-American and the Outstanding Player of the Pacific Eight Conference during his junior year. As Stanford's quarterback, Plunkett led his team to a victory over Ohio State in the Rose Bowl during his senior year. He went on to win the Heisman Trophy as the best college football player of the year.

The New England Patriots drafted Plunkett to play for them in 1971. He struggled during his first few years in professional football because of injuries. Plunkett joined the Oakland Raiders in 1978. He led the Raiders to a Super Bowl victory on January 25, 1981. Plunkett was named Most Valuable Player (MVP) of the Super Bowl and was also named Comeback Player of the Year in 1981. He led the Raiders to another Super Bowl victory on January 22, 1984. Jim Plunkett decided to retire from football after the 1986 season.

Quarterback Jim Plunkett won the Heisman Trophy as a college player before being drafted as a professional in 1971.

SELECTED LATINO SPORTS FIGURES

BASEBALL
Roberto Alomar (born 1968)
Felipe Alou (born 1935)
Moisés Alou (born 1966)
Luis Aparicio (born 1934)
George Bell (born 1959)
Bobby Bonilla (born 1963)
Bert Campaneris (born 1942)
José Canseco (born 1964)
Rod Carew (born 1945)
Orlando Cepeda (born 1937)
Roberto Clemente (1934-1972)
Dave Concepción (born 1948)
Tony Fernández (born 1962)
Andrés Galarraga (born 1961)
Cito Gaston (born 1944)
Pedro Guerrero (born 1956)
Vernon "Lefty" Gomez (1908-1989)
Juan González (born 1969)
Keith Hernández (born 1953)
Al López (born 1908)
Juan Marichal (born 1937)
Saturnino Orestes Armas "Minnie" Miñoso (born 1922)
Raul Mondesi (born 1971)
Tony Oliva (born 1940)
Rafael Palmeiro (born 1964)
Luis Tiant (born 1940)
Fernando Valenzuela (born 1960)

BOXING
Michael Carbajal (born 1968)
Bobby Chacón (born 1951)
Oscar de la Hoya (born 1973)
Sixto Escobar (born 1913)
Carlos Ortiz (born 1936)
Manuel Ortiz (1916-1970)
José Luis Torres (born 1936)

FOOTBALL
Manuel José "Manny" Fernández (born 1946)
Tom Flores (born 1937)
Joe Kapp (born 1938)
Max Montoya (born 1956)
Anthony Muñoz (born 1958)
Jim Plunkett (born 1947)
Fuad Reveiz (born 1963)
Tony Zendejas (born 1960)

GOLF
Nancy Lopez (born 1957)
Juan "Chi Chi" Rodríguez (born 1934)
Lee Trevino (born 1939)

HORSE RACING
Braulio Baeza (born 1940)
Laz Barrera (born 1924)
Ángel Cordero, Jr. (born 1942)
Laffit Pincay, Jr. (born 1946)
Jorge Velásquez, Jr. (born 1946)

SWIMMING
Pablo Morales (born 1964)
Tracie Ruiz (born 1963)

TENNIS
Rosemary Casals (born 1948)
Gigi Fernández (born 1964)
Mary Joe Fernández (born 1971)
Richard Alonzo "Pancho" Gonzales (born 1928)
Pancho Segura (born 1921)

TRACK AND FIELD
Alberto Salazar (born 1958)

Time Line

1871	Esteban Bellán is the first Latino to play major league baseball in the United States
1901	Luis Castro is the first Latino from South America to play major league baseball in the United States
1934	Lefty Gomez, a pitcher with the New York Yankees, leads the American League in strikeouts, earned run average (ERA), and wins; he repeats this performance in 1937
1934	Sixto Escobar wins the National Boxing Association bantamweight title
1939-1947	The Washington Senators have nineteen baseball players from Latin America on their team
1943-1945	Pancho Segura is the men's NCAA Individual Champion in tennis at the University of Miami
1948	Pancho Gonzales wins the United States National Championship in men's tennis; he wins the title again in 1949
1949	Minnie Miñoso becomes the first Latin American of obvious African ancestry to play on a major league baseball team
1956-1964	Luis Aparicio leads the American League in stolen bases
1958	Alex Olmedo of Peru is allowed to play on the U.S. Davis Cup tennis team and helps the team capture the Davis Cup title
1958	Ismael Valenzuela rides Tim Tam to victory in two important races: the Kentucky Derby and the Preakness
1961	Roberto Clemente of the Pittsburgh Pirates wins the first of four National League batting titles; he also won in 1964, 1965, 1967
1962	Carlos Ortiz wins the lightweight boxing title
1963	Braulio Baeza rides Chateaugay to victory at the Kentucky Derby and the Belmont Stakes
1963	Juan Marichal of the San Francisco Giants pitches a no-hitter against the Houston Astros
1964	Tony Oliva of the Minnesota Twins wins the first of three American League batting titles; he also won in 1965 and 1971
1965-1968	Braulio Baeza is the leading jockey in annual winnings
1965-1968	Bert Campaneris leads the American League in stolen bases
1966	Roberto Clemente is named the National League's Most Valuable Player (MVP)
1967	The women's doubles team of Rosemary Casals and Billie Jean King wins the first of five Wimbledon tennis titles
1968	Lee Trevino wins the first of two U.S. Open Golf titles; he wins again in 1971
1969	Rod Carew has a batting average over .300 for the first of fifteen consecutive baseball seasons; he also wins the first of seven American League batting titles
1969	Mike Cuéllar of the Baltimore Orioles wins the American League Cy Young Award for being the league's best pitcher

1971	Lee Trevino wins his first British Open; he repeats his victory in 1972
1970-1974	Laffit Pincay, Jr., is the leading jockey in annual winnings
1971	Jim Plunkett of the New England Patriots is named American Football Conference (AFC) Rookie of the Year
1974	Bobby Chacón wins the World Boxing Council (WBC) featherweight title
1974	Ángel Cordero, Jr., rides Cannonade to victory at the Kentucky Derby; Cordero rides the winning horse in two more Kentucky Derbys
1975	Pelé plays for the New York Cosmos of the North American Soccer League (NASL)
1978	Laz Barrera trains Affirmed, that year's Triple Crown-winning horse (winner of the Kentucky Derby, the Preakness, and the Belmont Stakes)
1980	Alberto Salazar wins his first New York Marathon; he wins again in 1981 and 1982
1981	Tom Flores coaches the Oakland Raiders to victory in the Super Bowl; after the team moves to Los Angeles, he coaches them to another victory in 1984
1981	Fernando Valenzuela of the Los Angeles Dodgers is the first major league baseball player to be named National League Rookie of the Year and to receive the Cy Young Award for being the league's best pitcher
1981	Jorge Velásquez rides Pleasant Colony to victory at the Kentucky Derby and the Preakness
1981	Rafael Septien leads the National Football Conference in scoring
1982-1984	Laffit Pincay, Jr., rides the winning horse in three consecutive Belmont Stakes
1984	Willie Hernández of the Detroit Tigers is named American League Most Valuable Player and receives the Cy Young Award as the league's best pitcher
1986-1989	José Santos is the leading jockey in annual winnings
1989	Pat Valenzuela rides Sunday Silence to victory at the Kentucky Derby
1990	Fernando Valenzuela pitches a no-hitter against the St. Louis Cardinals
1991	Julio Franco of the Texas Rangers wins the American League batting title
1992	Juan González of the Texas Rangers leads the American League in home runs; he leads the league again in 1993
1992	Oscar de la Hoya is the only American boxer to win a gold medal at the Summer Olympics in Barcelona, Spain
1992	Mary Joe Fernández and Gigi Fernández win the gold medal in women's doubles for the United States at the Summer Olympics in Barcelona, Spain
1992	Pablo Morales wins the gold medal in the 100-meter butterfly for the United States at the Summer Olympics in Barcelona, Spain
1992 & 1993	Cito Gaston, the first black Latino manager in major league baseball, manages the Toronto Blue Jays to consecutive World Series championships
1994	Oscar de la Hoya captures the World Boxing Organization (WBO) lightweight title
1994	Raul Mondesi of the Los Angeles Dodgers is named National League Rookie of the Year

GLOSSARY

backhand: A tennis stroke in which the back of the player's racket hand is facing the net when the ball is hit.

bandana: A scarf worn around the neck by cowboys. Cowboys often wore bandanas over their mouths and noses while they rode to avoid breathing dust.

bantamweight: A weight division in boxing for fighters who weigh 118 pounds or less.

caddy: A person who carries a golf bag full of clubs and other items a golfer needs to play golf. Caddies who work for professional golfers provide them with advice and tips on winning.

chaps: A pair of leather leggings that are worn over a cowboy's blue jeans to protect his legs. Chaps are usually fastened at the waist by a belt.

charrería (cha-rray-REE-ah): A rodeo competition with various contests.

correr el gallo (co-RRER el GAH-yoh): A rodeo contest in which riders pick up a small object from the ground while riding their horses at full speed.

earned run average (ERA): A statistic that tells how many earned runs a baseball pitcher allows every nine innings. The total number of earned runs are divided by the total number of innings pitched, and the resulting quotient is multiplied by nine to determine the ERA.

featherweight: A weight division in boxing for fighters who weigh 126 pounds or less.

flyweight: A weight division in boxing for fighters who weigh 112 pounds or less.

forehand: A tennis stroke in which the palm of the player's racket hand is facing the net when the ball is hit.

fútbol (FUT-bowl): The Spanish word for soccer.

hacienda (ah-cee-EN-dah): A large estate or plantation owned by Spanish settlers in the New World; also the main house found on such an estate.

jai alai (high ah-LIE): A popular racquetball game played with a large scooped-out paddle.

matador (mah-tah-DOOR): A person who fights a bull in a bullfight.

mestizo (mes-TEE-soh): A person of mixed Spanish and Indian heritage.

placekicker: A football player who kicks the football to score extra points after a touchdown.

pok-ta-pok: A ball game played by

the ancient Mayan people.

quarterback: The player who directs a football team's offense by signaling the plays they will make to score points. He is the main player responsible for passing the ball.

rancho (RRAN-cho): A Spanish word for a large cattle ranch.

reata (rray-AH-tah): A Spanish word for the rope or lariat used to lasso cattle, horses, or other ranch animals.

soccer: a popular game in which players try to kick or move a round ball into their opponents' goal, using any part of the body except the hands and arms.

vaquero (vah-KAY-roh): A Spanish word for cowboy.

welterweight: A weight division in boxing for fighters who weigh 147 pounds or less.

MORE ABOUT LATINOS AND SPORTS

Beezley, William H., ed. *Hispanic American Sports*. Radford, Va.: North American Society for Sport History, 1986.

Buck, Ray. *Jim Plunkett, the Comeback Kid*. Chicago: Children's Press, 1984.

Gilbert, Thomas W. *Roberto Clemente*. New York: Chelsea House, 1994.

Kanellos, Nicolás, ed. *The Hispanic-American Almanac*. Detroit: Gale Research, 1993.

Krich, John. *El Beisbol: Travels Through the Pan-American Pastime*. New York: Prentice-Hall, 1989.

The Latino Olympians: A History of Latin American Participation in the Olympic Games, 1896-1984. Los Angeles: Caminos Magazine, 1984.

Littwin, Mike. *Fernando Valenzuela, the Screwball Artist*. 2d ed. Chicago: Children's Press, 1991.

Morse, Charles. *Pancho Gonzales*. Mankato, Minn.: Amecus Street, 1974.

Oleksak, Michael M., and Mary Adams Oleksak. *Beisbol: Latin Americans and the Grand Old Game*. Grand Rapids, Mich.: Masters Press, 1991.

Wheelock, Warren, and J. O. Maynes. *Hispanic Heroes of the U.S.A.* St. Paul, Minn.: EMC Corp., 1976.

INDEX

Aztecs   7-8, 19

Ball games, types of   6
Baseball   10-14, 34-35
Bellán, Esteban   11
Boxing   15-18, 37
Bueno, Maria   26
Bullfighting   9

Casals, Rosemary   26
Charrería   20
Clemente, Roberto   13, 34-35
Cordero, Ángel, Jr.   22, 37-38
Cowboys   19
Cuban Baseball League   10

De la Hoya, Oscar   37

Escobar, Sixto   17

Fernández, Manny   30
Fernández, Mary Joe   27
Firpo, Luis Angel   17
Flores, Tom   29
Football   29-30, 40

Golf   30-32, 39-40
Gomez, Vernon "Lefty"   12
Gonzales, Pancho   25, 38
González, Miguel   12

Heisman Trophy   40
Horse racing   21-23, 37

Incas   8

Jai alai   9
Jockeys   21-23, 37

Kentucky Derby   38

Lopez, Nancy   32, 38-39
Luque, Adolfo   12

Marquess of Queensberry rules   15
Matador   9
Maya   6
Mexican League   12
Miñoso, "Minnie"   13
Morales, Pablo   32-33
Muñoz, Anthony   30

Negro Leagues   13

Olmedo, Alex   26
Olympics   27, 32-33, 37
Oropeza, Vicente   21
Ortiz, Manuel   18

Pelé   29
Pincay, Laffit, Jr.   23
Plunkett, Jim   29, 40-41

Ramírez, Raul   26
Rodeo   19-20
Rodriguez, Chi Chi   30-31

Salazar, Alberto   32
Sardiñas, Eligio   17
Soccer   9, 29
Super Bowl   29-30, 41
Swimming   32-33

Tennis   24-27, 38
Track and field   32
Trevino, Lee   30, 39-40

Valenzuela, Fernando   35-37

Wimbledon   26